# Dividend investing

# A beginner guide

# By Richard Smiths

# Table of Contents

# Introduction

I want to thank you and congratulate you for downloading the book, Dividend investing.

This book contains proven steps and strategies on how to  get started quickly on the path of dividend investing and ready to hit the ground running.

Dividend Investing is an investing approach where money is invested in stocks, bonds, mutual funds for seeking dividends that are regularly distributed to invest in the form of either cash or extra shares. Dividend Investing has over the time served investing community very well thru  various up or down market cycles with lesser risk and helped investors accumulate wealth over a period of time.

There is no easier way to achieve financial independence than to make more money while spending less. This principle has held true for generations and will continue to do so for years to come. What you do with the money you save is even more pivotal. Savvy individuals choose to invest it. Understanding different avenues of investing is pivotal to ensure your success in personal finance and towards your retirement.

If you are a beginner, be a young kid on the block, young or middle age or retiring women or man, and want to learn how to start dividend investing, this book is for you and will guide you with step by step instructions in easy to understand language without too much gibberish and hold your hand while you start your happy journey towards building a rich dividend portfolio. It's never too early or too late to begin this path,but you need to start now for your own rich life to enjoy.

You will get exact and reliable information in regard to the topic and issue covered. The book is sold with the information that the publisher is not necessary to render accounting, officially acceptable, or otherwise, professional services. If information is necessary, legal or acceptable, an experienced individual in the profession should be ordered.


Thanks again for downloading this book, I hope you enjoy it!

# Chapter 1    What is Dividend Investing

The dividend investing is considered one of the best ways for investors to collect steady and consistent returns. There are several people who invest in these dividend stocks to take advantage of that dependability before use some of those incoming funds to invest back into more shares of stocks – kind of like playing with some house money after winning a few rounds of blackjack at the casino.

Dividend investing is seen as one of the strategy that has become a savior in this economic environment by providing dividends through rain or shine. Power of dividends coupled with the compounding effect can produce hefty gains without taking too much risk and Ponzi schemes.

Many studies have found the effectiveness of dividends investing over a period of time. In fact, dividend investing could potentially empower you with rule of 36, rather than rule of 72, where investments could double in half time, if properly applied.

In case of dividend portfolio, asset allocation and diversification using a right mix of stocks/ETFs/Funds is paramount. As with any portfolio, there will be some risk elements, but the goal is to minimize them. With high rewards, come higher risks and therefore, goal is to achieve decent returns with less risk using dividend investing. Diversification of assets significantly determines the outcome of the portfolio success, not the timing of the market according to various pundits.

There are companies that pay consistently increasing dividends are usually considered financially balanced, generating a dependable return on investment on the distinct dividends. Stable companies generally feature any slipping stock prices to generate it less alarming to the shareholders in the overall market. Because of this, they can be considered less of a risk compared to the companies that don't sell out those dividends as well as, in turn, see more sharp good and bad in the value.

With a lower risk to the investors of these kinds of dividend stocks, they might be a more beautiful option for various investors – the actual young bucks who're hoping to obtain more income over the long term and for those who are looking to produce their retirement pay for. There are even those already in retirement who use money from dividend investing to supply a regular earnings while they aren't doing the work.

Another reason the particular dividend stocks get built confidence among dividend investors will be the correlation between the actual share prices and also the yield of gains through the dividends. When one rises, the different flows. There's also the consideration to the power of compounding the investments – having the generated cash flow and putting them on the stocks which will continue to build an increasing number of.

In other text, the money you have generated from your earnings will generate additional earnings and also the generations of producing earnings will carry on and follow as an investor continues to reinvest for time. This process may hypothetically turn one penny right into a very large sum of cash after about every thirty days.

If you take that particular penny and carry on and double your account each day for 30 days and nights, you could see your hard earned money grow from a number of cents to a couple dollars. Ten US dollars becomes $20, which often becomes $40, then $80, $160,

$320, $640, nearly thousands and gradually millions. Sure, there are many things who have to happen, plus it requires a minor luck. But theoretically, it can happen – regardless of whether it's a tad unrealistic.

This isn't expressing that any investor can get to see their particular money grow when realize use dividend trading. But it shows that money can, as well as likely will, grow in a process that Albert Einstein when called the eighth wonder from the world.

Many who enter the entire world of dividend investing might find the eventual rise of their rate of return because they continue to reinvest your money that comes of their returns to purchase.

Let's say you have 100 shares of a stock that offer at $50 every share – an investment around $5, 000. During that first year, the organization offers a 3. 5 percent dividend, to provide an income involving $125.

If the investor continues to see dividend growths involving 5 percent annually, that's a $5, 000 initial investment will be valued at just greater than $11, 200 after about two decades. This is while using the assumption that there will be no change in the stock price and there exists the reinvestment mentioned earlier.

Now let's get that same organization pay a quarterly dividend as opposed to one that pays annually. That's $5, 000 investment can grow to a tad bit more than $11, 650 with the same two decades to get a gain of about 133 percent. With the process of compounding, a $50, 000 investment can become an $116, 500 sum after that same stretch of time during which you will find reinvestments into the actual dividend folder.

# Chapter 2   What is dividend growth

Dividend growth is an important statistic for the investors. The stocks where have high dividend yields are frequently attracted by the investors.

But  what is the more important rather than the current size of the dividend is the pace at which it has been shrinking.You can see, the Growing dividend is a sign of good stock, which is committed to its stockholders. It is also a sign of more dividend, raise to come.

To see if there have any  problems, perhaps the stakeholder's needs to dig a little deeper into the company's financial Dividend Growth Rate, While a shrinking dividend or which is over-sized and it can be considered as a warning sign of problems with the company.

## Dividend Growth Rate

As with promises a big dividend means the stock's value has recently downed. To make the dividend income more without an increase in the actual amount of dollar in the dividend.

You can  see, the dividend growth amount is the average rate of growth and  stock's dividend has experienced for a certain period of time.

Depending on who's doing the analysis, there are numerous times periods you can use. But the phrase used must produce a statistic to help determine the best thing about owning a stock option.

A one hundred-year typical dividend growth rate seriously isn't a very applicable statistic. However, a five-year typical dividend growth rate could be spot on.

With regard to dividend growth price, a stock using a long history associated with dividend payments is usually admirable and may make the stock more desirable. But a newer history of both equally dividend payments and increases is often a better indicator with the stock potential dividend payouts for the coming years.

In addition to, of course, awareness is always critical to investment success. So research your options and calculate some sort of stock's dividend growth rate before you make an investment.

## Compound Annual Growth Rates (Cagrs)

When thinking about dividend growth rates over many years, it is proper and useful to do with compounding account, as opposed to a simple average growth rate. When looking at growth rate information, be sure to distinguish between growth information that uses compounding as well as growth data that could not do and so. The only way to make certain about this is to consider the actual every year figures (which may differ, and then calculate an example growth rate when using the formula for CAGRs. This formula is usually somewhat difficult to complete manually,so it is best to use a web site to compute CAGRs for you.

## Problems With CAGRs

Compound annual growth in costs will reflect this compounded growth right from the start of a time frame to the end. Any variation in growth rate during this time will not be reflected in this particular measure. The CAGR would be the rate at that a dividend could have grown if this had grown with a steady rate. Since hardly just about any investment grows at the exactly same rate each year, the CAGR might possibly be characterized as a great "imaginary" number. The true point is of which any variation within growth rate over a long time is definitely not reflected through the CAGR.

Dividend Growth Committing uses rolling five-year CAGRs over a reasonable length of time frames (preferably 20 years) to detect the two average CAGR as well as any variation within dividend growth rates through this period.

## 6 Advantages of Dividend Growth Investing

1. Allows an investor to get Get Paid to Wait

2. Dividend Growth Compounding

3. Take Advantage of Bear Markets

4. Capital Preservation

5. Create an Income Stream

6. Inflation Hedge: the income stream doesn't grow is the big disadvantage of fixed income investment.

## Dividend Growth Investing Strategy

The benefits of a dividend growth investing strategy allow it to be an important a part of portfolio management. Getting paid to await, dividend growth compounding, gaining from bear markets, capital preservation, a frequent income stream, and the opportunity to maintain purchasing power are extremely advantages of dividend growth investing strategies.

# Chapter 3 What is DRIP (dividend reinvestment plans)

Dividend Reinvestment Plan (DRIP) is a plan where the dividends that are received automatically reinvest in the underlying stocks/mutual funds/ETFs to acquire more stocks/MFs/ETFs, which in turn will earn more and so on, till the vortex of dividends will set in motion avalanche of cash flow for your whole life.

The dividend is a part of earning income that is distributed to the stakeholders when an organization makes profits. It is important to choose a good solid company that has a wide moat, as Warren Buffet says, at the right price. Dividends reinvesting unleashes the dual force of compounding magic as well as dollar cost averaging, due to the reinvesting of dividends, resulting in a significant accumulation of wealth over a period of time.

## DSPP (Direct Stock Purchase Plan):

Direct Stock Purchase Plan (DSPP) is a plan where an investor can purchase the stocks directly from the company without any commissions or fees. These plans are normally handled through transfer agent who administers them and will charge a very nominal fee. For e.g. Computershare and BNY Mellon manage DRIPs and DSPPs from hundreds of companies, including large and blue chips. DSPP plans allow you to reinvest the dividends, similar to DRIP plans.

# Chapter 4   The advantage of DRIP

Dividend reinvestment plan(DRIP) is  a cost effective way to put your dividend dollars to worthy use. Instead of  spending the dollars or having it sit in a bank account, the money can often buy more stock. Almost all of the programs allow dividends being reinvested for simply no fee. In the rough market, this is a terrific way to buy shares for a lower total price                                           tag.

Participating in the dividend reinvestment plan forces that you buy stock often. If you're signed up for a DRP, your cash will automatically end up being reinvested. As an end result, with very little effort, you'll adopt a long term horizon for your investments.

Almost all DRIPS carry a solution called optional income purchase. These allow investors to get additional shares for the nominal fee. Many optional cash buy plans have lower minimum investment needs. Some you can spend money on with as low as $10. Maximum investment limits vary based on the plan, though usually that figure reaches to the thousands.

One disadvantage regarding DRIPs is you must keep track of the cost basis on your individual purchases and observe after your own files. If you never have a lot of work if you ever attempt to sell the stock and must pay tax on your gains.

# Chapter 5   How to Retire through Dividend (living off dividends)

The biggest reason anyone wants to get into the world of investing – especially in the dividend sector of the market – is usually so that they can make enough money to cover the expenses that come with retirement. So there's a lot that has to be done to prepare for that day you decide you don't want to do a full 40-hour work week anymore, which starts with deciding which strategy to go with and then fine tuning it as the market changes over time (because what works now may not work the same way in 20 years).

How to reach those goals is focused on the type of dividend investing that generates a good cash flow for multiple decades, and that's easy done by following these guidelines.

## Always Contribute to Your Portfolio

The first rule is in order to continuously add money into your dividend profile, preferably some out of every paycheck or a greater amount every month. What happens is actually that investors are allowed to average the expense of their value over the course of several years.

This provides to be able to build a dividend folder stone by brick of which doesn't require the need to purchase all of your current stock in one single lump sum – which often isn't always the best option for those looking forward to retirement.

If people ignore it, then the benefits are limited as they are only building  is already right now there, and even though you will find there's reinvestment option, you'll be able to stand to make all the more money faster with the help of more into your investments. Think about that when you get that third cup of coffee shop brew that you simply average per morning.

## Seek Out a Dependable Dividend

The second rule is to maintain a focus on dividend growth stocks, which come from companies that usually offer a consistent raise of rates in distribution to the shareholders. If you want to have your dividend payouts cover your expenses while you are relaxing on the beaches of Maui, then you will want to have a dependable company to invest in for those long periods of time.

That's why investors attempt to find ways to avoid the risk of inflation and put their money in stocks that they can afford to increase their payouts on if they ever need to.

## Buy Quality - Not Necessarily Quantity

This task is bringing the savings into a brokerage account pertaining to additional investments, which means a good investor should build a collection of standard screening criteria so that you can have a report on dividend leaders as well as achieves – this is long unless you are able to trim the list to some more manageable amount.

One of what considered is in case a company offers a lot more than 2. 5 percent, dividends that have observed rises for at the very least 10 years in a row and trading under 20 times already in the market. While some may pun intended, the larger payout ratios – indicative that the company is benefiting a produce spike that won't last for a longer time (you wouldn't much like the dip on this roller coaster) – which could change with respect to the industry the company you happen to be potentially investing falls under.

Quality can become determined after careful research from the details for each stock which helps the investor figure out whether the stock options offers enough to provide a rising revenue rate and correlating dividend obligations over more than just a couple of years, but at least some decades. A properly diversified portfolio will provide good success for the different income stocks which you carefully picked. Speaking of which.

## Create a Diversified Portfolio

This is done so that you can not only to lessen the risk of loss, but to shield the investor by means of purchasing stocks from numerous different companies as you can for a far more steady income that will come in during retirement. You don't want to keep all your eggs in one basket, as this old saying is going. Some experts consider an investor's stock portfolio should include almost 30 individual companies which are scattered across many industries.

Think of a retail center and the amount of stores one usually has. They don't just have restaurants or department stores. There are specialty stores for gaming fans, photography folks, craftsmen, sports supporters, baby clothes, toys and almost everything in between. Would a mall using 20 or 35 Starbucks sound extremely fun? It likely wouldn't be extremely successful.

## Reinvest Wisely

When it comes to putting your money back into your dividend portfolio, don't do it too soon, and let your dividends build up. This is where the power of compounding interest comes into place where you are gaining more money in a shorter time. Not everyone uses that strategy, and most will likely hold their money for safer reinvestments and keep them with the steady growths.

# Chapter 6   How to Build a Dividend Portfolio

When it comes to investing in any form of the market, prior knowledge benefits investors the most in their efforts to save for retirement as they work and grow. No one should try to play a sport without having knowledge of the game – otherwise they will not be adequately prepared and will be quickly overtaken by the sharks in the water.

When building a portfolio of dividend stocks, an investor needs to know how to build an income and how it will help cover those financial needs long after you had that retirement celebration at the office where everyone congratulated you for your years of service. This doesn't mean you need to find a get-quick-rich scheme because investing in dividends is something you should plan to have working for you for a few decades – which requires knowing where to start and how to set up a dividend portfolio.

## Knowing the Risks of Inflation

Keep in mind that the possibility from the market's risk of inflation – the sustained increase from the prices on goods and services inside economy over a longer time of time – can impact different companies in numerous ways, depending on how much of a direct impact those larger expenses have on exactly where you invest.

There are a variety of risks that have to be kept in mind and weighed against each other when making individuals investment decisions. Experts usually topic themselves to both inflation as well as the market risk concerned, and the amount there're involved varies dependant upon how much they diversify their dividend collection. It's a challenging dilemma for everyone who invests while trying to find a dependable income with the long road ahead of time.

For example, a $1 million portfolio with a 5 percent rate usually provides an investor with in relation to $50, 000 on a yearly basis in income that will protect an investor with the aforementioned market possibility. But let's say make fish an inflation rate regarding 3 percent causes the investor to help only have in relation to $35, 000 of getting power about 12 years later. If you put in a tax rate of about 30 percent which $50, 000 then becomes about $25, 000 at the end of 12 years

## Benefits of Market Growth

So then, why would you choose to invest in dividends? Just about every portfolio on the market has its own set of risks—even non-guaranteed dividends and other economic risks like the one mentioned a few graphs above where there was a healthy dividend paying list of equities with a 4 percent yield.

Usually these have a payout that increases at least 3 percent each year and covers the inflation rate, possibly growing 5 percent annually over those same 12 years. If the latter were to happen, then that $50,000 you started with would grow to about $90,000 each year, but would be about $62,000 after the planned 3 percent inflation rate. Let's say there is a 15 percent tax (which is always something that can change later on) makes that amount worth about $53,000.

When a portfolio is able to combine both of those methods, it is able to defend itself against the negative effects of inflation and any fluctuations in the stock market. Being able to have a diverse portfolio that includes stocks and bonds is a good way to make a dependable income that won't be affected too much by the potential dividend hazards.

## Steps to Building a Dividend Portfolio

### 1. Create Diversity in Your Portfolio with at least 25 Solid Stock Options

This isn't about trying have King Solomon's gold by starting with nothing. Smart investors remain centered on the long-term goal of experiencing money to fund money during retirement, and that takes time along with patience. Receiving dividends work better focus and besides stock growth and never having to accept a company's possibility.

### 2. Diversity among Multiple Industries

The right choice means not putting all of your beans in one single pot. For example, if all of your stocks come from different oil companies, it would be a shame if the price per barrel fell as much as $10 or more and would make a negative impact on your dividends. One way of avoiding that dreaded dividend cut is to spread your selections out.

## 3. Financial Stability is More Important than Growth

Obviously, if the investor had an alternative C for the exam, they might select that you for "both A and B. Which can be a tough thing to try and do, so the 1st priority in the investor is to focus on having far more dependability which means that your company will provide dividends in which increase over time rather than relying upon the prospect of quick growth. This may be accomplished by keeping track of each company you might potentially buy by watching their credit ratings. The Value Line Investment decision Survey commonly grades these types of stocks via A++ and entirely down to the Ds and focus on stocks together with 'A' ratings for your least volume of risk.

## 4. Look for Companies That Have Modest Payout Ratios

Those ratios are calculated from the dividends as a percentage of the total earnings. If a ratio is 60 percent or less, it means the company has a lot less wiggle room when there could be some unforeseeable trouble down the road. It's best to invest in a company that has a plan for what to do to protect their shareholders in case of any economic crisis.

## 5. Reinvest What You Earn from Your Dividends

This goes back to the power of compounding that we have talked about in a few of the earlier chapters. By putting the money earned into investments well in advance of when you may need the money for that retirement, the dividends could result in a very surprising amount of growth that doesn't require too much of an effort from the part of the investor.

## The Biggest Mistakes to Avoid When Growing Your Portfolio

A big reason why dividends are looking more and more attractive to investors these days is because the yields and bonds are stressfully low, and investors who are looking to plan for their eventual retirement are looking towards dividend-paying stocks for a more dependable income that builds efficiently over a longer period of time.

Dividend investing has become a popular strategy during a time where fixed-income is falling into lows that haven't been hit before and the baby boomer generation is preparing to enter the world of retirement.

That's not to say there isn't any sort of pitfalls, as with anything in the stock market during tough economic times. There are a number of catches in the face of all of the good things that dividend portfolios bring—a list of about seven according to San Francisco advising company, Forward Management, in a report titled How Not to Invest in Dividend Stocks.

## Relying on Overly Mechanical Investment Plans

These kinds of strategies often ignore basic shifts as well as dividend policy changes, which could build a problem for the investor's dividend profits flow. This has happened a few times in Europe where many of the telecommunication companies that will paid via benefits had higher makes that had increased beyond completely – which, mentioned previously earlier, is a danger sign that things are planning to go down because what climbs up must come down.

## Ignoring a Variety of Growth Factors

Profitable investors have to see and evaluate not only the dividend yields that every company has settled, but also what the company's potential is made for both growth and appreciation – expansion is what allows someone every single child have more settled to them over a longer period of time, which often can help them keep a livable income when they join the old age community.

For illustration, let's imagine that an investor has any portfolio with $1 million and would like to withdraw about $50,000 per year for expenses like home, food, and so forth. If the trader earns about 3 percent in whole returns, less than 1 / 2 of the starting equilibrium would remain after two decades. Another 10 years later, that same trader earning only 3 percent could well be close to jogging out. Now if in which same person was able to grow their returns to about 7 percentage, they would have savings of about $3 million there after same 30 year period.

## Showing Favoritism to the Home Market

There are many options overseas in other countries which have the booming economy that are paying dividends which have higher averages, that are obviously more positive to investors in addition to sometimes provide better options the United states.

Investing in the particular global market has developed into very important factor in the ability to diversify a portfolio by such as industries in those people fast-growing markets. By way of example, people are beginning move cloud surgical procedures overseas to African countries since the demand is increasing there such as Amazon in addition to VMware. In 20 years, those markets get increased there shares in the world economy and are the cause of about 47 percent in the world's gross home product.

## Focused Towards Those Blue Chips

Investors sometimes claim there's more safety in having those larger dividend stocks, but they also cost more to buy shares and won't offer as much in return as they once did than the ones that are smaller or middle of the road in cap size. Those larger companies usually offer a liquidity advantage but still don't offer a lot of opportunities to see increased dividend yield.

Investor demand has risen so much that those blue-chip stocks are becoming too costly to even consider as options for a diverse and successful portfolio.

## Giving Macro Factors More Weight

There's always about to be plenty of risks with regard to any form regarding investing—it's inevitable as you'll find emerging markets that supply some intriguing probable – especially involving troubled nations along with possible booms in Europe, the Middle East and Africa. Those regions may provide a large number of international revenue benefits and local operations which might be less of times be affected by macro trends.

For example, the stocks from the European market aren't becoming valued as highly due to current crisis which in turn causes doubt for buyers. But there is still a chance to find some stronger companies that offer dividend payments in that part of the world that might provide some potential gains that can help your portfolio.

# Chapter 7   How to Rebalance Your Portfolio

Being able to rebalance a dividend portfolio can be an extremely useful way to remove the emotions an investor may have when they make their decisions regarding the ups and the downs of those holdings. Successful investing comes from making smart, diverse decisions that are meant for the long haul, meaning as an investor, you have to be diligent, patient, and willing to stick to your plan rather than look for quick cash.

## Establish Your Targets

First, you can start with targets of what is important to like in the dividend portfolio. Having these focused sectors usually works the very best, especially if you're an investor who would like to have up to 30 and up different stocks. While it might be hard to target everyone stock, it's better to spotlight each industry and base your individual decisions on their performance afterwards.

How many you end up picking in each sector is your decision as an entrepreneur – sometimes you need to invest in 10 diverse companies, and sometimes you simply find a couple of. It all is dependent upon how comfortable the investor has been that industry. But concurrently, it's important never to put each of the eggs in 1 basket – you will need a diverse dividend portfolio for top investment success.

One example is, you decide that your particular portfolio will develop the following sectors manifested – financial (15 percent); resources (15); telecommunications (15); power (10); healthcare (10); real estate (10); retail items (10); technology (5); community transport (5); in addition to bonds (5). finance institutions like banks, along with utilities that provide for the public and also telecommunications due to the growing need for mobile technology. The rest are of interest to this hypothetical investor – however while playing it safe given that they feel their bigger cuts develop the best chance to create consistent gains.

## Select a Rebalancing Trigger

While some investors use a new once-a-year trigger, many investors usually prefer to see the different stocks into their portfolio more generally than an once-a-year checkup many specialists will recommend one or more times every quarter, if not more. That's because there are so many fees which are linked with buying and selling that you wouldn't want to miss the opportunity to do either along with cost yourself some a lot of money.

Giving yourself about three months to generate a move is generally acceptable because you don't necessarily want to be too hasty in the event that a company which had one minor dip one month could bounce back another. There's an old expression that goes "sell in May and go away" – which is like a warning to sell stocks in the month of May to avoid a potential periodic decline that occurs out there before returning inside the full swing in November when numbers begin to increase again.

Another trigger that lots of investors use is establishing a portion variation for each sector that may decide the rebalancing of one's dividend portfolio. Should your target is to get 10 percent in transportation, you could transfer it 3 percent one of many ways or the other and then, you could decide to sell or buy shares in this sector. The challenge originates from not just modifying one sector but the need to adjust the other six you keep – some experts recommend while using the option to sell with the cash or make investments additional funds.

## Take a decision How You Will Rebalance Your Portfolio

Rebalancing a dividend portfolio doesn't mean that the investor has to sell stocks. Sometimes it's just easier to only add funds as a matter of planning how to rebalance the percentages among the sectors in a portfolio.

An investor usually wouldn't sell 10 stocks that are worth $100 and then paying the $10 commission fee because it just doesn't make much sense. Rebalancing your dividend portfolio might not be possible in an efficient manner and requires a large amount of planning before any type of decision is made – remember, working with a dividend investment portfolio means no hasty decisions.

Let's say this hypothetical portfolio, we have mentioned earlier is worth more than $100,000 and most of the investments have at least $5,000. Trades are made worth $1,000 that makes the aforementioned commission fee look really small in comparison – that's considering the 10-20 percent differential target within your portfolio.

## Do So within Each Sector

Keep an eye on each of the sectors represented in your dividend portfolio and analyze whether anything needs to be changed internally and not as much on a broad scale. If you own stocks in six banks under the financial sector, there might be an opportunity to rebalance between a few of them based on when you bought the stocks.

Eventually, the stocks that are doing well will need to be sold for a profit that can then be reinvested in the other existing banks in your portfolio. Or you could add a couple of other companies that have shown some great potential for making your portfolio even stronger. Usually when an investor makes this type of decision, they are putting their money in a bank that is providing stronger, more consistent yields as opposed to one in their portfolio that wasn't pulling its weight.

Some experts would recommend waiting until the stock has reached a certain point above the original purchasing price – like around the 20 to 25 percent point. Then an  investor is recommended to evaluate the time needed to build that profit and compare it to the other stocks in the portfolio.

# Conclusion

Thank you again for buying this book!

I hope this book was able to help you to know about the Dividend Investing.

Finally, if you enjoyed this book, then I'd like to ask you for a favor, would you be kind enough to leave a review for this book on Amazon? It'd be greatly appreciated!

Thank you and good luck!

www.ingramcontent.com/pod-product-compliance
Lightning Source LLC
Chambersburg PA
CBHW071544170526
45166CB00004B/1551